Original title:
Maple Tree Memoirs

Copyright © 2025 Creative Arts Management OÜ
All rights reserved.

Author: Julian Carmichael
ISBN HARDBACK: 978-1-80567-228-9
ISBN PAPERBACK: 978-1-80567-527-3

The Dance of Seasons

In a park where trees sway and giggle,
Leaves whisper secrets, they wiggle and wiggle,
Squirrels perform their acrobatics,
While falling leaves make ridiculous antics.

Autumn arrives with a colorful show,
Donning a scarf made from leaves in a row,
The wind plays tricks, gives hats a neat pull,
As we chase acorns, our laughter is full.

Winter sneaks in, wearing white fluffy coats,
Frosty faces and snowball fight gloats,
Snowmen with noses made from old carrots,
Yet, they all melt, creating new parodic merits.

Then spring bursts forth in a hoppy parade,
Flowers dance wildly, in hues none have made,
Beehives do cha-cha, with energetic buzz,
While the grass tickles toes, oh what a fuss!

Summer sizzles, we jump in the pool,
Ice cream drips down, it's a sticky old rule,
With laughter and joy, we're light on our feet,
And under the sun, every day feels sweet.

The Golden Path to Reflection

Beneath the boughs, where squirrels leap,
And acorns roll, my thoughts run deep.
I ponder life and all its quirks,
How nature shines, while chaos lurks.

The sunbeams dance on golden hue,
Each leaf a tale, both old and new.
I chuckle at the trees' grand jest,
For nature knows how to invest.

With every breeze, a giggle flows,
As branches bend with secret woes.
I tip my hat to those who dare,
To climb the heights, not just despair.

So here's my toast to all that's odd,
Embrace the weird, give fate a nod.
With laughter echoing through the grove,
We'll weave our tales in joy and love.

A Legacy Woven in Leaves.

In each rustling leaf, a story lies,
Of clumsy kids with pie in their eyes.
They climbed the heights with hopes so bold,
Each fall was worth the tales retold.

The wind would tease, toss hats away,
As laughter filled the autumn day.
With every crunch beneath our feet,
The legacy of fun's complete.

Oh, how we danced in nature's grace,
With goofy moves and silly face.
Each moment shared, a vibrant thread,
A tapestry of joy we've spread.

So let us shout, let echoes ring,
For all the joy that leaves can bring.
We'll treasure each whimsical embrace,
And laugh as time can't steal our space.

Whispers of Crimson Leaves

The leaves are blushing, ever bold,
Each one a secret, a tale retold.
They gossip softly in the breeze,
About our mishaps and little tease.

From picnics planned to karaoke stars,
We've sung so loud, we're heard from Mars.
With every flutter and awkward fall,
The trees just laugh, they've seen it all.

With squirrels stealing snacks for a toast,
They gather round, a merry host.
Their chittering song, a hearty cheer,
A chorus of memories, loud and clear.

So here's to laughter, crisp and bright,
With every leaf, a spark of light.
We'll dance through autumn with joy and glee,
Embracing whispers of living free.

Autumn's Tapestry

As nature paints her grand facade,
With brushstrokes wild, though not too awed.
We frolic where the colors blend,
Creating tales that never end.

With pumpkins dressed in silly hats,
And playful ghosts and goblin chats.
The grass beneath our happy feet,
Serves up adventures, pure and sweet.

In every pile of leaves we dive,
The joy we share keeps dreams alive.
For every laugh in fiery hues,
A memory's stitched into our shoes.

So lift a glass to autumn's show,
With humor rich, and hearts aglow.
We'll weave our tales, a vibrant string,
In life's great tapestry, let's sing!

The Canopy of Change

In the fall, the leaves take flight,
They swirl and dance, what a sight!
Squirrels giggle, chasing their tails,
While I trip on my shoelace trails.

The branches wave like a silly hand,
Whispering secrets, oh how they stand!
A gust of wind sends my hat on a spree,
And the birds all cackle, 'Look at me!'

Echoes in Amber

A golden hue amidst the green,
Nature's artwork, a funny scene.
Jumping in piles, I hear a crack,
Was that a leaf or my old backpack?

The laughter rings through the crisp air,
As squirrels plot more than just despair.
Chasing their dreams of acorn glory,
While I slip and stumble, but it's a fun story!

Secrets Beneath the Bark

Underneath, the mysteries lie,
In knots and grooves where insects fly.
The wise old bark gives me a wink,
As I ponder what these critters think.

The riddle's clear, but I'm a fool,
Guessing the gossip is just plain cool.
Like a gossip queen in a leafy disguise,
Spilling the tea to the passing flies!

A Symphony of Gold

When autumn sings, it's quite a tune,
With rustling notes under the moon.
Leaves fall like confetti in a bash,
While I make an impressive splash!

The chorus of crunches fills the park,
I trip and fall, oh what a lark!
As nature chuckles in vibrant hue,
I'm just grateful I wore my rubber shoe!

Whispers of Autumn's Embrace

A squirrel wearing a tiny hat,
Chased his nuts in a comical spat.
Fallen leaves did a silly jig,
While birds laughed at the dancing twig.

Pumpkins strutted in random delight,
Mice held a party, oh what a sight!
The sun laughed as it began to fade,
Sharing secrets in a sunlit parade.

Each gust of wind told a cheeky tale,
Of acorns that dared to set sail.
They rolled down hills like little cars,
Heading home from far-off bars.

In this bright season, joy does swell,
With crunching sounds, all is well.
Laughter echoed through fields that gleam,
As nature danced in a whimsical dream.

Crimson Leaves and Forgotten Dreams

A leaf tried to spin, but it tripped,
Fell down with a flop, and it lip-synced.
Buddies laughed as they rolled on by,
In the theatre of trees, oh my, oh my!

There once was a crow with a knack,
For fashion; her feathers were bright and black.
Draped in a scarf made of old hay,
She strutted like she owned the day.

Dreams of harvest danced in the air,
While corn stalks waved without a care.
The scarecrow snickered, boots to the sky,
He looked so dapper; oh me, oh my!

Underneath the boughs, a debate,
What's better, a snack or a blind date?
Yet every whisper turned into cheers,
As nature toasted to autumn's years.

Beneath the Canopy, Shadows Dance

Beneath the branches where giggles reside,
A raccoon claimed the best spot to hide.
He wore shades and sipped on a brew,
Says, "This autumn's the best view!"

A fox in a sweater tried to impress,
But tripped on his tail—oh, what a mess!
Laughter erupted from bushy-tails near,
As they whispered secrets for all to hear.

Rain clouds joined in with a playful pout,
But found themselves laughing, there's no doubt.
They tossed out sprinkles for fun and flair,
Until puddles formed for a splashy affair.

In these moments, shadows take flight,
Jumping and twirling till the night.
With critters giggling in twilight's glow,
They shared the wonders of autumn's show.

Echoes of a Turning Leaf

The whispering wind had a cheeky tone,
As a leaf hitchhiked, not wanting to moan.
He waved goodbye to his limb so tall,
Shouting, "Catch me if you can, y'all!"

Tiny critters held a falling fest,
Rolling down hills, oh, weren't they blessed?
Each flip and flop brought out the joy,
Even the toads leapt like a buoy.

The cooler air brought a ticklish feel,
As pumpkins giggled over their last meal.
Ghosts in the corners sighed in relief,
For costumes awaited in a playful brief.

Autumn's antics danced on repeat,
With laughter echoing down every street.
Yearning for laughter, the trees joined in,
As leaves spun tales of where they've been.

The Secrets of a Sturdy Bough

In a park where the squirrels dance,
And acorns tumble at every chance,
A sturdy bough creaks with delight,
Telling stories of squirrelly flight.

Its leaves gossip in the brisk breeze,
Whispering secrets through the tall trees,
About the time a bird took a dive,
And how it barely survived the jive.

With each branch holding a tale to share,
Of picnics, laughter, and sun-kissed air,
It chuckles at the antics below,
As kids play tag in a wild flow.

So if you sit under this jolly frame,
You'll hear laughter, and whispers of fame,
For every bough has a secret or two,
That'll tickle your heart and giggle with you.

Warmth in the Cool of Fall

When leaves turn gold and carpets are made,
I wear my sweater, so bright, so frayed,
The chill bites quick, but I laugh and run,
Playing tag with shadows, oh what fun!

The crunch beneath my clumsy feet,
Like nature's laughter, a crunchy treat,
Each step's a giggle, a silly song,
But who needs grace? I'm where I belong.

The wind throws colors into the air,
While I attempt to twirl without a care,
It pulls my hat off, watch it soar,
As I chase it like a child wanting more.

So here's to fall's playful, golden spree,
Where warmth rises in laughter, wild and free,
I'll build a fort of leaves, just you wait,
And celebrate life in this autumn state.

In the Heart of the Orchard

In the orchard, apples bounce and roll,
Daring me to take a bite for the soul,
I pick one up, just a bit too ripe,
And toss it high, hoping for a snipe.

The trees are gossips, their branches sway,
Sharing old tales of the fruit's ballet,
Of a shy pear who dreamed of the sun,
And a curious plum who just wanted fun.

I trip on roots, but laughter takes wing,
As I plop down with a giggle and fling,
The colors of harvest swirl all around,
In this silly labyrinth, joy is found.

So join the dance 'neath the harvest moon,
Where laughter grows, and smiles make room,
For every blunder's a story to tell,
In the heart of the orchard, all is well.

A Tapestry of Amber Dreams

The world turns amber with each fading light,
And dreams weave tales in the soft, sweet night,
I pull on my blanket, cozy and bright,
While my thoughts take flight, a whimsical sight.

With crickets chirping their midnight tune,
And stars playing tag with the friendly moon,
I giggle at shadows that wiggle and roam,
In the fabric of night, I feel right at home.

Each leaf that flutters is a secret to find,
Some silly, some funny, and perfectly kind,
A tapestry spun from the yarns of delight,
Promising laughter till dawn's golden light.

So let's drift through dreams, with whispers and glee,
Where the world is a canvas, just you and me,
In this tapestry of amber, we'll play and weave,
Crafting our stories in nights that believe.

When Sunlight Fades

When sunlight fades to golden glow,
The squirrels take over, their acorns in tow.
Chasing each other with wild, silly glee,
In this odd ballet, they're the stars, you see.

Beneath the branches, all snug and tight,
Bumblebees snore from morning till night.
The shadows stretch long, the laughter won't cease,
In this quirky world, there's always a peace.

Cradle of Autumn's Heart

In the cradle of autumn, we dance and fall,
While pumpkins conspiring wink just to call.
The winds whisper secrets, it's all a charade,
As leaves play tag in this vibrant parade.

A raccoon steals snacks while the crows look askance,
Lamenting they missed the best party of chance.
With each silly slip, we all burst with cheer,
And capture such moments, delightful and dear.

Leaves as Letters

In a breezy post, leaves flutter and fly,
Each one a letter, they giggle and sigh.
"Dear Summer," they write, "it's cold as a bear!"
With ink from the sky, they send joy everywhere.

They gossip and chortle, "What's next in our tale?"
As swirls of bright colors rock dance in the gale.
Crickets giggle, "We'll join in the fun,"
With each little breeze, there's laughter for everyone.

Seasons of Our Story

Seasons shift fast like a well-timed joke,
While afternoons linger with mischief and smoke.
We pile on the leaves, making forts and more,
But the cat's the real boss, guarding her score!

Sweaters and hot cocoa become our best friends,
As we fend off the chill, the laughter never ends.
With stories we weave, both silly and bright,
In the seasons of stories, we find pure delight.

The Language of Bark

In the woods where whispers dwell,
Each tree has tales it loves to tell.
With cracks and knots, a secret code,
In the bark, their stories flowed.

Squirrels claim their leafy crowns,
While birds exchange their silly sounds.
A chipmunk munches on a snack,
While ticks in trees just plan their hack.

Beneath the shade of leafy green,
The quiet bumblebee is seen.
With every rustle and every cluck,
Nature's court is full of luck.

So listen close to each tree's lore,
There's humor in their barky score.
From silly nuts to acorn fights,
The forest's jest is pure delight.

Glimmers of Every Season

Spring brings blooms and pollen flurries,
While the bees dance without worries.
Summer laughs with sunshine bright,
Ice-cream drips and feels just right.

As autumn sways, leaves tumble down,
It's a colorful party in this town.
Winter greets with frosty glee,
Snowmen giggle under a snowy tree.

Each season spins a playful tune,
With jingling frost and pansies in bloom.
So grab your friends, come take the ride,
In nature's joke, let's all abide.

Autumn's Embrace

Squirrels scamper with nuts galore,
Harvest time, we all adore.
Pumpkins grin with orange hue,
Trick or treat, oh, how they brew!

Leaves that crunch with every step,
In vibrant colors, we all prep.
The air smells sweet, yet crisp and bold,
Whispers of warmth from days of gold.

Candied apples and cider cheer,
Ghosts play pranks and give a scare.
Autumn's dance is wild and free,
A playful jest from nature's spree.

Reflections on the Forest Floor

Upon the ground, where leaves do lay,
A carpet of colors makes us stay.
Mushrooms peek and laughs abound,
Nature's jesters on the ground.

Pinecones drop with little thuds,
An acorn rolls, oh what a dud!
Each step reveals the forest's grin,
With secrets held, we're drawn within.

Beneath the trees, all creatures play,
Each critter has its fun display.
A symphony of rustles and cheeps,
In this wild theater, laughter leaps.

Roots of Remembrance

In the yard where we played, so bright,
We'd climb up high, just to take flight.
Branches like arms waving hello,
Giggles like bubbles, they'd float and flow.

The leaves whispered secrets, oh so sly,
Of funny mishaps when we'd touch the sky.
Falling with flair, in ungraceful spins,
Laughter erupted, where silliness wins.

Under its watch, childhood thrived,
Each knot in the trunk like a joke, derived.
We'd snack on the fruit while swinging our feet,
Old stories echoed, a whimsical treat.

Roots intertwine, our memories blend,
Under its shade, we'd twist and bend.
With every rustle, a wink from the past,
In the embrace of nature, childhood was vast.

Dancing with the Winds

The breeze had a jig, we joined in the fun,
Spinning and twirling, oh what a run!
Branches were partners, they swayed and pirouetted,
While we stomped our feet, delighted, half-witted.

Squirrels rolled by, with acrobatic flair,
In the dance of the dappled light, we'd twirl in mid-air.
Leaves were confetti, bright colors in flight,
We laughed in the sunlight, hearts feeling light.

Dancing with shadows, we jumped to the beat,
Every step silly, no need for retreat.
Losing our footing, we'd tumble and fall,
Yet laughter would echo, bonding us all.

The winds told their tales, of mischief and play,
As we leaped and we twirled, chasing clouds all day.
In nature's grand ballroom, with joy we would spin,
A lesson in laughter, let the fun times begin!

A Canopy of Confessions

Under the leaves, we made silly vows,
To tell all our secrets, like silly old cows.
Eyes wide with wonder, ears perked so tall,
We giggled in whispers, sharing it all.

A chorus of chuckles, our jokes intertwined,
With roots as our witnesses, laughter enshrined.
Confessions so goofy, of crushes and dreams,
In the shade of the branches, all bursting at seams.

Nature was our stage, a theatrical show,
Each blush and each blunder, like props in the flow.
From floors made of grass, to the skies so wide,
Under this canvas, we'd all laugh and bide.

We'd vow to come back, to share more with glee,
No secret too silly, for our leafy decree.
With smiles like sunshine, we'd dance until night,
Walking away home, with the humor still bright.

Laughter in the Orchard

In the orchard we roamed, with puns in the air,
Fruits giggled softly, all ripe for a dare.
Grapes rolled with laughter, as apples would tease,
Banana jokes slipped, like leaves in the breeze.

We chased after shadows, our giggles took flight,
Snickering at squirrels, what a comical sight!
Peaches, they whispered, "Don't take us for fools!"
As we cracked up a storm, with our silly ol' rules.

Every twig snapped underfoot like a drum,
Our folly would echo, it made us feel numb.
The joy would erupt like bubbles in soda,
Ripe laughter and fun under fruity locomotion.

As the sun dipped low, we shivered in fits,
The orchard our playground, our funniest bits.
With each fruity giggle, a memory's made,
In this laughter-filled haven, we joyfully played.

The Stillness Between Seasons

In the quiet, squirrels dance,
Chasing dreams of nutty chance.
Leaves whisper secrets, oh so spry,
While acorns plot a silly lie.

Frosty mornings, a fuzzy hat,
Worn by a raccoon chasing a cat.
Birds argue over a twig in a tussle,
Nature's sitcom, a comical hustle.

Sunlight beams with a playful wink,
As I ponder on the brink.
Is winter here, or just a joke?
Ice cream dreams, with a maple bloke!

Oh, what lie does spring soon tell?
When flowers trip, they do it well.
In the stillness, laughter hums,
With nature's pranks, oh here it comes!

The Golden Sway

Blowing breezes tease the leaves,
Tickling branches, what a breeze!
Golden hues of sunlit cheer,
Rustling giggles, loud and near.

Dancing shadows play all day,
As I chase them, hips in sway.
The grass is giggling, join the fun,
While I trip over roots, oh what a run!

Fallen leaves, a crunching sound,
Jumping in piles, joy unbound.
Every splash, a laugh so bright,
As autumn wraps us in delight.

With a swoosh and a woosh, I glide,
Falling leaves all around in pride.
Who knew the ground could be so spry?
Underneath the golden sky!

Hearthstone Reflections

The fireplace crackles with glee,
As shadows dance, just like me.
Hot cocoa spills, oh what a mess!
I laugh it off, my own success!

Fuzzy socks on chilly toes,
A game of hide and seek with crows.
The cat rolls in a patch of sun,
Where did I leave that last bit of fun?

Comfy chairs and tales retold,
Of woodland creatures brave and bold.
Footprints in the snow so bright,
Were they mine, or a friend's delight?

In the warmth, antics sway,
As old jokes begin to play.
Each chuckle echoes through the night,
In hearthstone laughs, we all unite!

A Journey Through Canopies

Up high where the breezes tease,
An adventure through the towering trees.
I stumble on branches, swing side to side,
With birds gossiping, oh what a ride!

A summit view, what a sight,
Where bugs engage in a ten-legged fight.
Clouds scatter like cotton in pairs,
And I question if they've left any airs.

Rustling leaves tell tales of old,
Of owls and raccoons, both brave and bold.
Each twist and turn invites a giggle,
A forest full of laughter's wiggle.

Through sunlight patches, I weave and spin,
Where do rocks and laughter begin?
In nature's lap, a skip, a hop,
In this world of whimsy, I can't stop!

Letters from the Wind

The wind whispers secrets, silly and light,
Chasing squirrels who scurry from fright.
A gust sends a leaf right into my stew,
I wonder if veggies would like a zoo too?

With each swoosh and swirl, a giggle is heard,
Dancing with laughter, just like a bird.
A paper plane flew, but made a huge flop,
Guess the wind just wanted to make it stop!

When autumn arrives, it wears a bright grin,
Leaf confetti rains down, oh where do I begin?
Crispy crunch sounds, like popcorn on air,
While pinecones gossip without any care.

So here's to the wind, our mischievous friend,
With letters of laughter that never will end!
Each twisty tale floating by is a treat,
Served fresh by the breeze, oh life is sweet!

When Leaves Speak in Colors

Once upon a time, leaves had a chat,
In hues of bright yellow and vibrant sprat.
'I'm feeling so orange,' said one with a grin,
'Next week, I'll flaunt my deep russet skin!'

'I love when the kids jump in a big pile,'
Chimed in a leaf with a cheeky smile.
But the reds, looking posh, proclaimed with flair,
'We make it look classy, so do take care!'

Amid the green chatter, a bold leaf declared,
'Fall's just a giggle, and winter's impaired!
Let's roleplay as snowflakes, fancy and white,
To trick all the children—what a delight!'

As the sun dipped low, they glimmered in hue,
Colorful giggles danced off the dew.
With nature's stage set, what a colorful sight,
The leaves had conspired—now isn't that right?

A Canopy of Laughter and Grace

Up high in the branches where squirrels convene,
A canopy teems with stories unseen.
'Hey, what's that rustle?' a leaf whispers wide,
'Just those pesky tourists who can't seem to hide!'

The owls share chuckles about nighttime games,
While raccoons roll dice with their ridiculous names.
A whirl from the wind nudges some sap,
Who giggles and drips as if taking a nap!

In the shade of their laughter, sunshine doth beam,
Beneath, a green blanket in nature's sweet dream.
Upon every branch, the jesters provide,
With laughter so rich, it can't be denied!

When storms come a-knocking, they hold on so tight,
Waving their arms, they bid the clouds light.
Oh, what a gathering, what fun to embrace,
In this leafy old world of laughter and grace!

Seasons of Life in Every Grain

In spring, the buds spring forth with a tease,
'Look at us grow!' they laugh in the breeze.
Each little blossom a whispers apart,
Tickling the boughs like a cheeky dart.

Summer tosses in a sun-soaked play,
Leaves dance to music, no time to delay.
Picnics and laughter, the children will cheer,
'Don't crumple the snacks, or we'll shed a tear!'

When autumn arrives with a crackle and pop,
Pumpkin spice jokes make the laughter just hop.
'How many leaves does it take for a fall?'
'Enough for a yearly leaf pile to call!'

Winter brings ice that sparkles like cheer,
Laughs in the snowflakes that glide without fear.
With every season, the joy never wanes,
In nature's grand tapestry, humor remains.

Harvesting Memories from the Ground

In the yard, I found a shoe,
It belonged to a kid—who knew?
Mismatched socks, oh what a sight,
Tree roots giggle, oh what a night!

Toys and trinkets buried deep,
A hidden treasure, barely a peep.
Each object tells a silly tale,
Of squirrels plotting a cheeky scale.

Caterpillars dance with flair,
While acorns hide without a care.
I swear that one gave me a wink,
Next to the bucket where they drink!

Nuts with hats, oh what a show,
Chasing each other, to and fro.
As chaos reigns upon the ground,
Funny memories abound, profound!

Beneath the Harvest Moon

Under the glow of a big round pie,
Frogs croak songs that make me cry.
Worms throw parties in a pile,
While I just stand and watch for a while.

Moonbeams dance on apples bright,
The raccoons laugh, oh what a sight!
Each sparkling fruit, a jest they share,
With dancing leaves that twist in air.

Scarecrows gossip with a crow,
About the plants they did not sow.
A pumpkin tried to steal the night,
But tripped on roots and lost the fight!

I joined their party, laughing loud,
A fruit salad mixed with a cloud.
As laughter blooms beneath the stars,
We hold our memories like sweet Mars bars.

Autumn's Palette in Twilight's Glow

Brushstrokes of orange, yellow, red,
Nature paints while we laugh instead.
A leaf fell down with quite a thud,
And started a riot in the mud!

Giggling squirrels with cheeks so fat,
Steal acorns while wearing a hat.
They're planning a nutty parade,
While autumn's colors serenade.

Pumpkin faces all around,
Some frowning, some upside down.
Each carved line tells a funny joke,
While beneath them, old leaves choke.

Twilight whispers, "Let's have some fun!"
As shadows dance, we all become one.
In this canvas, memories twirl,
A whimsical autumn, in laughter, we whirl!

The Journey of a Simple Seed

From dirt to sky, what a grand dream,
A little seed with a laugh and a gleam.
It stumbled along, no map in sight,
Only sunshine and worms for delight.

Through puddles deep, and mud so thick,
Each step felt like quite a trick.
"Grow up tall!" the whispers urged,
As around it, critters converged.

A bug said, "Here's a secret, friend,
Watch out for storms that might bend!"
But our seed winked, "I'm built for this,
With time and laughter, I'll find my bliss."

So up it went, through laughter and cheer,
A dance with the wind, no hint of fear.
And in the end, with roots so grand,
It waved to the world, a proud little stand!

The Dance of Changing Colors

Leaves twirl in the autumn air,
A squirrel slips, without a care.
Orange and gold, a vibrant show,
Spinning round like they're in a disco!

Birds wear coats of funky hues,
Chirping tunes that bring good news.
The ground's a canvas, painted bright,
As critters join this silly sight.

Coffee cups spill, laughter's near,
As dancers sway without a fear.
The world's a stage, in this tight-knit crew,
Where even the shy leaves learn to break through.

In swirls and rustles, joy takes flight,
Each gust of wind, a pure delight.
With each color shift, a jest unfolds,
A leafy tale that never gets old!

In the Shade of Giants

Beneath the giants, the picnic spreads,
Ants march in lines, ignoring our breads.
The sun peeks in, then hides away,
While squirrels discuss their acorn play.

A laughing child throws crumbs afar,
Ducklings quack like they're rockstars.
"Hey, look at me!" the baby shouts,
As ice cream melts, the chaos sprouts.

Shadows dance like silly fools,
While we sip lemonade from colorful tools.
The tree trunks whisper their tales of yore,
While we create memories to adore.

Giggling branches sway in delight,
As friends gather under the soft twilight.
In the shade, laughter's a sweet embrace,
In the heart of nature, we find our place!

Fragments of Sunlit Days

Sunbeams catch in a playful game,
As laughter shatters the awkward fame.
Each moment's a puzzle, a silly mix,
Where lemonade stands are our old tricks.

In the glow, butterflies tease bees,
As grasshoppers hop with comical ease.
Frisbees fly with wobbly spins,
While we chase after our childhood wins.

Laughter echoes, a bubbling brook,
As shadows hide in a cutesy nook.
We build our castles from sunlit rays,
In fragments of these whimsical days.

The air is sweet with memories bright,
In goofy dances, our hearts take flight.
Together we sing, with voices bold,
Creating fragments more precious than gold!

The Shift of Shadows

Watch as the shadows shift and sneak,
Each one tells a jest, so to speak.
They trip and tumble, they giggle low,
As we wander through this nature show.

A dance of pixels across the grass,
While squirrels debate who's first to pass.
Leaves catch whispers, secrets unfold,
With every rustle, a tale is told.

The sun rolls down, time does a spin,
While shadows chase, plotting their win.
"Catch me if you can!" they playfully shout,
As the light dims, they twist about.

In the quiet dusk, laughter lingers,
As our own shadows wave, like happy fingers.
In this twilight, joy's always near,
With shadows that dance and never disappear!

Shadows of the Past

Beneath the branches, shadows dance,
I tripped on roots, lost my pants!
Squirrels chuckled, oh what a sight,
As I scrambled home, in pure fright.

Leaves were laughing, colors bright,
They whispered secrets of the night.
I mumbled tales of clumsy bliss,
Under the moon, not one thing missed.

Sapling Dreams

Little sapling, growing fast,
Wiggling in the wind, what a blast!
Plans for glory, branches wide,
But sunlight made you want to hide.

Dreamt of being a flag in the sky,
But now you're just a space for flies.
Catch the breeze, oh dear young sprout,
In your daylight party, shout it out!

The Rustling Chronicles

In the breeze, a story flows,
Of acorns falling, who really knows?
A dance of life, a rustling tune,
Under the watch of the bright moon.

Old leaves tumble, gossip in flight,
About the critters that roam at night.
Each crackle tells a tale so grand,
Of days gone by, and mischief planned.

Harvesting Memories

Gather around, it's that time again,
To share the laughter of foolish men.
Baskets brim with stories sweet,
Laughter echoes, feel the heat.

Picking fruits, but losing track,
Stumbling forward, now that's the knack!
Juicy tales, oh such delight,
As we treasure the harvest night.

The Rustle of Time in Every Leaf

In a forest of whispers, I stroll,
As trees gossip secrets, quite droll.
Each rustle a chuckle, a tease,
While squirrels play tag with the breeze.

The wind tickles branches, a joke,
While acorns debate with a stroke.
Laughter erupts from the bark,
A comedy show in the park.

Fallen leaves dance in a waltz,
With critters to blame for the faults.
A raccoon in shades steals the show,
What a fabulous, leafy glee flow!

So here in this canopy wide,
Time strolls along, cats at its side.
With each turn, a memory spins,
Oh, the joy that this forest brings!

Nostalgia in a Forest of Color

Amidst hues of amber and gold,
I recall tales the old trees told.
How laughter once echoed so bright,
Under leaves that twinkled at night.

A crow caws a punchline or two,
While butterflies flutter, adieu.
Each petal a postcard from the past,
Fleeting joys, forever vast.

The sun makes its entrance with flair,
While shadows play tricks without care.
A deer trips on its own dainty feet,
Oh, the antics of nature can't be beat!

So under this canopy's embrace,
I catch giggles sprinkled in space.
In every shade, a memory waits,
Oh, the fun that nostalgia creates!

Reflections on a Rustic Path

Along this path where laughter roams,
Old stones tell jokes while birds build homes.
With each step, a chuckle we share,
Nature's a clown, with a flair!

A frog croaks a tune from the bog,
While busy bees jive, quite the slog.
The sun peeks through, a joker in light,
Illuminating fun in sight.

Pine needles tickle with delight,
As I wander through day into night.
Each twist and turn, a comedic tale,
In this woodland, where giggles prevail.

So here I am, with nature's jest,
Finding humor in every quest.
In rustling leaves, and playful breeze,
Life is a laugh, oh so sweetly seized!

The Gathering of Golden Hours

As daylight fades, a gathering starts,
Trees shake hands, swapping their smarts.
With sunset's glow, jokes spread like seed,
In this hour, nature's humor we need.

Fireflies glow, like tiny lights,
Illuminating mischief-filled nights.
A gathering 'round, critters unite,
Who'll tell the best tale? Oh, what a sight!

Laughter bounces off trunks and leaves,
As wisdom flows from old oak eaves.
With each wink from the stars above,
Nature wraps us in giggles and love.

So let's bask in this golden hue,
With each chuckle, let's start anew.
For in this moment, all is clear,
Nature's jest is what we hold dear!

Nostalgia in the Breeze

The wind whispers secrets of old,
While squirrels dance, a sight to behold.
Chasing leaves like a feathered friend,
Time flies fast, will it ever end?

I recall days of lemonade sips,
And summer's laugh in carefree trips.
Yet here I stand, in rustling hues,
Wishing for a childhood with less to lose.

The Embrace of Fall

Autumn's blanket of orange and gold,
Worn by trees, so brave and bold.
They shimmy and shake in the crisp, cool air,
Declaring war on the coats we wear!

With every gust, a giggle erupts,
As acorns tumble and squirrels get abrupt.
They gather their stash, with such a flair,
While I trip over roots, my toes beware!

Threads of Time Entwined

In tangled roots lie tales of play,
Days spent roaming, making hay.
Each twisted branch a knot of cheer,
Recalling fears of growing up here.

With each rustle, a laugh resounds,
A memory formed that knows no bounds.
Nature's jokes float on the breeze,
Tickling cheeks, bringing me to my knees!

When Leaves Speak

Whispers of leaves in a lively chat,
Sharing gossip, so imagine that!
"Did you see Fred roll in that pile?"
"Oh, let's catch him in that goofy style!"

Under their boughs, the world grows absurd,
As laughter in colors feels like a bird.
With each gentle flutter and playful tease,
They remind us to giggle with utmost ease.

Tales from Beneath the Bark

In a hollow trunk, a squirrel snores,
Dreaming of acorns and forest tours.
A raccoon pops in, wearing a hat,
Yelling, 'Who's stealing my pretzel snack?'

Underneath the roots, bugs throw a bash,
Dancing away to a funky clash.
But a worm slipped on a slippery leaf,
Now he's the punchline of the nightly grief.

Beneath the canopy, shadows disguise,
A shy little beetle with very wide eyes.
He tells a joke that's quite offbeat,
But everyone laughs at his wobbly feet.

So life flows on in this wooden world,
With giggles and troubles all mismatched and swirled.
From nuts to laughs, they enjoy the start,
In the realm of the trees, everyone's an art.

Roots of Resilience

The roots ran deep, though twisted and funny,
Living it up like it's big money.
An earthworm shouted, 'We're hip and cool!'
As moles played chess inside their school.

When drought would strike with sunshine's bite,
The roots held tight, they'd grip and fight.
'No water? No problem!' the crickets cheered,
'Turn up the heat, we've nothing to feared.'

In watery floods, the roots had their say,
'Turn this into a la-la parade!'
With splashes and laughter, the earth came alive,
Each bulb and twig began to thrive.

So here's to the roots, they know how to prank,
With jokes and jests as their leafy prank.
They wiggle and dance, and say with delight,
'We'll weather any storm and party all night!'

Wings of Change

A breeze blew through with a tickle and sway,
Whispering secrets of the day.
A leaf took flight, a whimsical show,
Twisting and turning, like a pro.

On a flapping wing, a brave little bug,
Practiced his moves, gave the world a shrug.
He landed with flair on a petal so slight,
Claiming, 'I'm Da Vinci, just taking a flight!'

Yet a gust popped in, quite hefty and bold,
Launching our artist out into the cold.
With cartoonish spins and a flurry of squeaks,
He landed in puddles, with messy techniques.

With laughter and cheers, they all took a chance,
Wings of change led to a jubilant dance.
In the air they swirled, no sense of defeat,
For every mishap was a new kind of treat.

Painted Skies and Fallen Glory

In the autumn glow, the colors bled,
Leaves did a jig, and the branches said,
'Let's have a party, we're dressed to impress!'
With shades so bright, it's anyone's guess.

But then came the winds, all frisky and sly,
Swooshing the leaves, tossing them high.
'Oh dear!' cried the hues, 'We're losing our crown!'
As they danced from the trees, twirling down.

They laughed at the ground, all glossy and bright,
'Today we'll be art, what a whimsical sight!'
With giggles galore, they piled in a heap,
Creating a masterpiece, no time for sleep.

So under the sky, painted fierce and bold,
Fallen victories spun stories untold.
Each leaf's little giggle, a golden delight,
In the canvas of nature, chaos feels right.

The Language of Winds and Whispers

The winds spoke softly, in breezy delight,
Whispering tales while taking to flight.
A burly old branch, quite grumpy and stout,
Yelled, 'Stop your chatter, I'm trying to pout!'

Yet the breezes just laughed, swirling the air,
'Your mood can't stick, it's too light to bear!'
The leaves wobbled nigh, giggling to the core,
As they shared secrets from the branch to the floor.

They'd snap and they'd crackle, their stories would twine,

In playful debates over closeness and vines.
'A leaf's just a sprout,' said a wise old crow,
'But together we thrive, just letting it flow!'

And so, with alliance, they rose from the bough,
Creating a chorus, a jubilant vow.
The language of whispers, both foolish and bright,
In the world of the woods, everything feels right.

Nature's Diary

In the park, a squirrel prances,
Chasing shadows, taking chances.
Falling leaves dance in the air,
I trip on one, without a care.

The grass is green, a little shaggy,
My dog rolls in it, getting braggy.
He thinks he's caught a little breeze,
But it's just bugs; we both sneeze.

A ladybug, bright as a light,
Lands on my nose, what a sight!
It tickles so, I laugh aloud,
A patch of ants, I'm quite the crowd!

Nature notes, they're all a jest,
Every sprout thinks it's the best.
But in this diary, one thing's true,
It's all a giggle, just like you!

The Colors of Yesteryear

Yesterday's hues were quite the sight,
Orange and yellow, feeling bright.
A kid with paint splashed on his face,
Brought the joy, a wild embrace.

We launched our kites, oh what a show!
One got stuck in the neighbor's crow.
They squawked and cawed, we laughed in glee,
A colorful chase, just kids and spree.

The sun set low, a golden gleam,
Sipping lemonade, we'd daydream.
Got sticky fingers, a pop's last fizz,
Those gentle days, such simple whiz!

Now memories fade like old paintbrush,
Clouds float by, in a gentle hush.
Though colors may blend and fade away,
The laughter echoes, come what may!

Roots that Bind Us

In this garden where we play,
A gopher's got something to say.
"Who planted this? It's full of weeds!"
But look at it, a patch of seeds!

With every bloom, a story found,
Of family ties, oh so profound.
Grandma's daisies, her prized delight,
Now just a battle with the night!

The petals dance, they tease the wind,
Telling tales that never end.
Roots intertwine like gossiping friends,
Digging deep where laughter blends.

So here we stand, a patchwork crew,
With dirt on our knees, an old shoe or two.
Who knew that weeds could bring such cheer?
A family garden, sincere, my dear!

Tales of the Verdant Past

Once upon a time, in forest green,
A hedgehog wore a crown, quite the scene!
He said, "I'm king of this leafy land!"
A squirrel replied, "You're not so grand!"

They argued and fumbled, rolled on the floor,
Until the grass squeaked, "Hey! No more!"
The daisies giggled, the trees swayed,
In the court of nature, hold court, we played.

A gust of wind blew all around,
And flipped their hats right off the ground.
"Oh dear!" they cried, in quite a fuss,
Chasing caps, they forgot all the fuss.

And in that moment, joy was shared,
As laughter echoed, they both declared:
In the thick of leaves, it's all about fun,
In this verdant past, together we run!

Woodland Whispers

Leaves giggle in the breeze,
Squirrels plotting mischief trees.
Acorns drop like tiny bombs,
Nature's jokers, how it calms.

Bugs dance in a wobbly line,
Sipping nectar, feeling fine.
Fungi wear their party hats,
Toadstools clapping, shaking stats.

Birds perform their silly songs,
Chasing tails till something wrong.
Pinecones tumble, what a sight,
Nature's laughter, pure delight.

Shadows play and shadows tease,
Rustling softly as they please.
Every rustle brings a grin,
In the woods, we all fit in.

The Weight of Growth

I tried to stretch my branches wide,
But found my limbs had too much pride.
With every gust, I'd sway and bend,
Looking for a leafy friend.

Sunshine warms my furrowed bark,
But on my limbs, a squirrel's park.
They're lounging high and feeling spry,
While I'm just here to sigh and try.

Roots dug deep, they claim the ground,
While ants march in, all around.
Beneath my shade, a picnic scene,
With crumbs of laughter, bread, and green.

If I could laugh, oh what a laugh,
With every ring, a photograph.
Who knew growing came with weight,
While juggling joy and mossy fate?

A Mosaic of Memories

Each leaf tells stories of the past,
Of windy days, and shadows cast.
With whispers soft, they make me smile,
Mapping laughter mile by mile.

A chipmunk's tail, a fleeting dance,
Moments captured in a glance.
The summer sun, a friend to all,
Old tales gather, how they sprawl.

Seasons change like costumes worn,
From vibrant hues to frayed and torn.
Yet in decline, there's joy to find,
In every crack, a tale entwined.

So here's to memories that rise,
Echoes of laughter fill the skies.
In every leaf that's fallen down,
A snapshot blooms, without a frown.

The Beauty of Decay

Look at me—I'm withered, bold,
A tapestry of stories told.
Fungi flourish, take the stage,
In my splendor, they engage.

Colors fade but joy remains,
Crunchy sounds like laughing chains.
Soft whispers from the ground do call,
Celebrating life's crooked sprawl.

Lichen hugs my wrinkled face,
Nature's art in this slow pace.
Every flake, a laughter shared,
In this journey, all prepared.

So raise a toast to fragile grace,
With every wrinkle, find your place.
In every twist, a seed is sown,
The beauty of decay has grown.

Remnants of Radiance

In autumn's fluff, I find a thrill,
Red leaves swirl, they dance at will.
Squirrels clutching acorns, oh what a sight,
Turning the ground into a woodland fight.

A gust of wind, the laughter rolls,
As leaves take flight, it fills the shoals.
Chasing colors, a joyful spree,
Who knew nature could be so zany?

Around the trunk, a raccoon prances,
With mischief bright, in leafy glances.
He steals my hat, oh what a tease,
Running away, he does it with ease.

Under trees, we reminisce and play,
Creating memories that never decay.
In every rustle, in every sway,
The remnants of laughter always stay.

Canvas of Change

Painting the sky with orange hues,
Leaves falling fast, we've got our cues.
Puddles reflect a goofy grin,
Splashing around, let the fun begin!

The artist's brush has gone a-roaming,
Colors collide, the senses foaming.
I slip on a leaf, oh what a joke,
Laughter erupts as I start to croak.

Nature's palette is wild, diverse,
Swirls of colors that hardly rehearsed.
Underfoot the crunchy sounds delight,
Every step a cause for pure excite!

As shadows lengthen, joy won't fade,
These playful moments are well replayed.
Reality's canvas, a laughter spree,
All thanks to the whimsy, wild and free.

Pinecones Underfoot

Pinecones scatter like dropped jewels,
An obstacle course for nature's fools.
We dodge and weave, it's pure delight,
Who knew that walking could spark such fright?

With every crunch, a giggle erupts,
Over the forest floor, mischief disrupts.
A pinecone missile, I take aim and throw,
But miss the target—squirrel says, "Oh no!"

A family of critters joins in the chase,
Over each other, they tumble with grace.
They scurry and dart, in the autumn gold,
Our comedy act, never gets old.

Falling leaves complete this lively dance,
We twirl and dive, caught in a trance.
Laughter abundant from root to crown,
Life's little joys, never let down.

Breath of the Wind

The breeze plays tricks upon my hair,
Whispers secrets, so light, so rare.
It tugs and pulls, a cheeky tease,
Dancing with willows, swaying with ease.

A gust arrives, my papers take flight,
Chasing them down sparks pure delight.
I stumble and fumble, what a grand show,
The breeze just laughs as it starts to blow.

Whirling around, it keeps us on toes,
In nature's embrace, laughter just grows.
With every rustle, a new tale spins,
Breath of the wind, where the fun begins.

So here we stand, in nature's playground,
With every twist and turn, joy is found.
Let's ride the currents, seize the day,
In the wind's warm laughter, we'll forever play.

Fragrance of Fallen Leaves

The leaves are falling, oh what a sight,
They dance in circles, much to delight.
Squirrels are chuckling, having a ball,
Diving and dodging, not worried at all.

Crunchy whispers beneath my feet,
Leaves in my shoes, oh what a treat!
A sneeze erupts, I blame the trees,
They giggle and shake with such eerie ease.

Nostalgic scents paint the air,
Remembering summers without a care.
But now we're laughing, in the cool breeze,
As trees tell secrets, if you please.

Autumn's a joker, with tricks up its sleeve,
Who knew such fun was hidden in leave?
So here's to the mirth, through laughter we weave,
In a world where we run, and never reprieve.

A Shelter from Time

Once stood a giant, in roots so deep,
A home for the critters, where silence could creep.
We'd hide beneath boughs, from the world so grand,
While breeze told us riddles, each grain of sand.

Tick-tock went the clock, but we stayed still,
Chasing shadows, with an unstoppable thrill.
Branches like arms, in a warm embrace,
Who needs a house when there's such grace?

The ladder once broke, oh what a fright!
The squirrels turned acrobats, full of delight.
We laughed at mishaps, made memories last,
With a wink and a grin, propelled by the past.

So here's to the shelter, our secret retreat,
Where time doesn't matter, nor work or defeat.
In the heart of the woods, we found our sense,
Amongst all the laughter, it all feels immense.

Amongst the Twirling Leaves

A whirl and a twirl, oh what a dance,
Leaves swirling 'round as if in a trance.
With each gust of laughter, they leap and dive,
The jests of the wind make them feel alive.

Who knew the fall could tickle so bright?
A carnival hosted by nature's delight.
The colors all jostle in a playful show,
As we burst into giggles, how quickly they go!

Wind plays the jester, with a whoosh and a blow,
Leaves float like feathers, all swaying to and fro.
We catch them and toss them, no worry today,
Just laughter and fun in this glorious display.

So come join the circus, beneath the sky's dome,
With leaves as confetti, and laughter our home.
We'll remember this moment, in jokes that we weave,
As we twirl with the leaves, in a world we believe.

Sowing Seeds of Remembering

In a pile of leaves, we burrow down deep,
Amidst the laughter, sweet memories creep.
Funky adventures, from summers long past,
Each giggle a seed, in our hearts amassed.

A treasure trove sparked by the crunching sound,
Tales of mischief and joy abound.
We shared secret whispers, beneath the tall hue,
Where time was a jest, just laughter anew.

Underneath the branches so grand and wide,
We'd map our escapades, each mishap a ride.
Joking and playing, till sun sank low,
Guessing the stories that only trees know!

So here's to the moments, like leaves on a spree,
With each burst of laughter, we sow memory.
In this garden of joy, with friends near or far,
We'll cherish the smiles, like leaves, they will spar.

Beneath the Canopy of Dreams

Underneath the leafy shade,
A squirrel thinks he's getting paid.
He tries to dance, trips on a root,
Leaves us laughing, what a hoot!

The branches sway, a rustling breeze,
An acorn drops with teasing ease.
"Catch me if you can!" it seems to shout,
Nature's game, there's never a doubt!

The birds gossip in chirps so bright,
Sharing tales from dawn till night.
All of them, a feathered crew,
Leave us wondering what is true.

Beneath this roof of playful cheer,
We chuckle at life, oh so dear.
With giggles shared under the sun,
Who knew that life could be such fun?

A Journey of Colors

Oh, orange, yellow, red galore,
Each leaf bursting, begging for more.
Falling down, like confetti from trees,
We dance around, with the autumn breeze.

A raccoon wearing a nutty hat,
Struts and prances, how about that?
He juggles acorns, a sight to see,
While laughing at squirrels up in the spree.

When twilight comes, shadows grow long,
And silly shapes sing a funny song.
We trip and tumble over the ground,
In this colorful playground, joy abounds!

Each step we take, a crunch and a crack,
Exploring the woods, there's no looking back.
With laughter echoing in the air,
A journey of colors beyond compare!

Stories Written in Leaves

Leaves whisper stories, secrets untold,
Of sunny days and nights so bold.
In their rustle, we hear a tune,
Of dancing shadows beneath the moon.

A ladybug, wearing polka dots,
Tells of mischief, it never forgot.
While ants parade in a line so neat,
In their tiny world, they can't be beat.

A feather drifts down, a tale from the sky,
Reminding us all that we can fly.
In this leafy library, laughter reigns,
As stories twist like the playful chains.

With each falling leaf, a giggle ignites,
In this woodland theatre, pure delight.
Nature's memoirs dance in the breeze,
Telling us life is meant to please!

Botanicals of Memory

A dandelion dreams of being grand,
While a clover plots with a whimsical plan.
Together they hatch a scheme so spry,
To tickle your toes as you walk by.

In the garden, a sunflower sways,
A gossip queen in sun-shiny rays.
She shares old tales of the bees' grand heist,
A sweet-scented treasure was the prize they sliced.

Amidst the petals, a laugh erupts loud,
A thinking toad, feeling quite proud.
He croaks his wisdom from way up high,
"Life's but a hop, so give it a try!"

With stitches of laughter sewn in the seams,
The wildflowers plot and share wild dreams.
In the botanicals where memories play,
We find the joy in every day!

The Dance of Transformation

Once a bud with dreams so bright,
In springtime's haze, a leafy sight.
Dancing leaves that twist and spin,
Sway with laughter, let fun begin.

A whirlwind of colors, gold and red,
Chasing squirrels while running ahead.
Whispers of fall, a crispy cheer,
Flip-flop hats for all who appear.

Winter's chill brings a frosty grin,
Snowflakes whispering tales of kin.
Nature's costume party, oh what a show,
Who knew trees could put on such a glow?

As spring arrives, the cycle starts,
Leaves giggle, maturing arts.
From bud to bloom, a waltz so grand,
The dance of life, a playful band.

Timeless Truths in Nature's Canvas

A canvas stretched where colors blend,
Secrets of nature, messages penned.
Brushstrokes of green, laughter anew,
A palette of wisdom, fun stuff to chew.

Rippling rivers run wild and free,
Telling tall tales, just wait and see.
Rocks chuckle low in shadows they keep,
Mossy whispers adding to their sleep.

In autumn's glow, crayon skies above,
Leaves gossip their stories, push comes to shove.
The canvas changes, a playful twist,
Nature's art, impossible to resist.

Time's tick-tock in the trees so wise,
Counting the laughs, the highs, the sighs.
Life painted vibrant, in colors profound,
Timeless truths, on this canvas, abound.

Echoing the Seasons of the Heart

Beats of spring and a fluttering soul,
Every new leaf plays a jolly role.
Squirrels chirping, their mischief bright,
Tales told in each sun's warm light.

Summer brings warmth, an overgrown spree,
Picnics and laughter under the tree.
Bees buzzing tunes, join in the fun,
Nature's concert has just begun.

Autumn's whispers, a ticklish breeze,
Crisp crunching leaves become a tease.
A parade of colors, it's quite the sight,
That coon in a hat, oh what a fright!

Winter rolls in with a snowman grin,
Bundled up tight, let the games begin.
Seasons echoing laughter, heart's wild art,
Life's mischief painted, a canvas to start.

Nature's Diary Under the Sun

Pages turning in the sunlight's embrace,
Each petal a word, a curious trace.
Nature's diary, filled with delight,
Wink of the flowers, oh what a sight!

Stories of raindrops, funny and sly,
Dancing on rooftops, painting the sky.
Birds with feathers like brushes in flight,
Sketching adventures, a pure, joyful sight.

Golden rays glimmer, the book's opened wide,
Frogs leap in verses, nature's own guide.
Crickets recite under stars' gentle glow,
Writing their sonnets, wait 'til you know!

As the sun sets on this playful tome,
Nature whispers secrets, far from home.
In the heart of each leaf, stories spun,
Nature's diary, alive with fun.

Vibrance in Shadows

In the garden, trees do sway,
Whispers dance with leaves at play.
Squirrels plot their grand escape,
Nuts they hide in a leafy drape.

Sunlight giggles through the boughs,
A chorus sung by nature's cows.
Frolicsome bugs join the fun,
While flowers blush in the sun's run.

Birds in suits demand a show,
Worms in ties move nice and slow.
Nature's carnival, quite the sight,
With furry beasts in sheer delight.

Branches wear a funny hat,
As a raccoon juggles a sprat.
Laughter echoes from the ground,
In this fiesta, joy is found.

At the Crossroads of Seasons

Winter peeks with frosty breath,
While pumpkins laugh with warm, soft heft.
Spring teases with a sunny wink,
But bees are busy in a drink.

Leaves are donned in colors bright,
A disco party, pure delight.
Trees gossip in a rustling tone,
As neighbors meet, they're never alone.

Hats made of foliage twirl in glee,
As critters play hide-and-seek, you see.
Frivolous wind gives a playful shove,
As branches dance, they fall in love.

Shadows stretch like stories told,
In nature's playhouse, bright and bold.
Where each season brings a jest,
And merriment is at its best.

Tides of Yellow

Golden leaves like laughter fall,
A rustling giggle, nature's call.
Squirrels dash in a dizzy chase,
In this wild and wacky space.

Sunbeams spill in cheerful sights,
Painting the world in warm delights.
Laughter echoes through the trees,
As critters join the buzzing bees.

Dancing in autumn's gentle grip,
Pumpkins roll in a humorous trip.
Each gust of wind, a playful nudge,
As kittens pounce and softly judge.

Rooted in fun, the branches twirl,
With each new leaf, a strange new whirl.
In the comedy of the grand design,
Nature concocts her favorite wine.

Chronicle of Changing Winds

Breezes whisper in a cheeky tone,
While leaves tumble like soft, sweet scone.
The laughter of gusts, a comical show,
As flowers sway and take a bow.

The dance-off starts when winds arise,
With silly trees in bright disguise.
A dandelion drifts, whimsical and light,
In a game that plays into the night.

Colors chat under a sunny sky,
As clouds form shapes that wave goodbye.
Giggling leaves share secrets deep,
In this tale of joy, they take a leap.

With every twist, nature's witty spin,
A snapshot of fun, where dreams begin.
In this chronicle, we find delight,
As seasons giggle into the night.

Beyond the Canopy

Up high in the branches, they chatter and cheer,
Squirrels joke loudly, it's their time of year.
They toss all the acorns, they play like a game,
While the old owls hoot out their humorous name.

With leaves like confetti, they dance in the breeze,
Falling like laughter, bringing joy, if you please.
The branches keep swaying, a comical sight,
As shadows of munchkins play tag with delight.

Where Memories Unfold

A raccoon in pajamas, sneaks out for a snack,
His fur all a-mess, but he's got no lack.
Underneath the bright moon, he tries out a jig,
While the fireflies giggle, they dance oh so big.

Old boots hang on branches, a sight to behold,
Left by a runaway with stories untold.
They whisper of mischief, of laughter and fun,
Reminding us all that the joy's just begun.

The Flora of Forgotten Times

Once in the forest, a flower gave speech,
Charming the toadstools with tales that they preach.
They talked of old parties where roots would unwind,
And how mushrooms once danced in circles they twined.

The vines were the gossip, they twisted and curled,
Spreading the laughter of that leafy world.
In every petal, a chuckle resided,
As nature's own humor in sunlight presided.

A Tapestry of Twigs

The twig people gather for a grand old show,
In costumes of bark, oh how they do glow!
They laugh and they frolic with whimsical grace,
As pinecones become stars in this quirky space.

With each chubby squirrel that stumbles on stage,
The audience roars, it's a comedy page.
Who knew in the forest such tales could arise,
Where laughter and timber are the ultimate prize?

The Last Laugh of Autumn

Leaves tickle the ground, a dance with glee,
Squirrels plotting mischief, a scampering spree.
Acorns are rolling, a clumsy sight,
Nature's comedy, pure delight.

Wind whispers secrets, a cheeky tease,
While critters debate, 'Is it time to freeze?'
Pumpkin heads grin with a hint of cheer,
As autumn chuckles, 'The end is near!'

Bark-covered benches, where friends congregate,
Sharing tall tales of a porcupine date.
The sun plays peek-a-boo, laughter erupts,
In this golden season, hilarity's cupped.

Cells of sweet laughter, they burst and soar,
As leaves twirl down, begging for more.
A playful farewell, the sky painted red,
With a wink, autumn whispers, 'Let's party instead!'

Unraveling Stories

Twisted branches weave tales of their past,
While birds chirp gossip, so colorful and fast.
Each rustling leaf has secrets to share,
Of chipmunks and frogs with foolish flair.

Mushrooms rise up in their polka-dot style,
As critters debate who's the funniest by a mile.
The old owl chuckles, feigning a yawn,
As world-weary leaves tumble and fawn.

Sunlight pours down, a golden embrace,
As shadows join in with a comical grace.
Every branch is a storyteller grand,
With a punchline waiting—can you understand?

Underneath the canopy, laughter resounds,
With nature's comedians bounding around.
The heart of the forest beams with mirth,
In the echo of autumn, joy finds its berth.

When Forests Breathe

Trees take a breath, expanding with glee,
Exhaling their chuckles like puffs of free tea.
Branches high five as the critters convene,
While squirrels debate who can leap green to green.

In the shade, the rabbits are plotting a play,
With carrots for props, they're prepared for the day.
While wise old toads let out raucous croaks,
Creating a rhythm for all earthy folks.

The breeze brings a tickle, leaves giggle and sway,
In harmony, creatures just dance and display.
Roots have a reunion beneath the still ground,
With whispers of laughter that echo around.

Nature winks knowingly, it's all in good jest,
As laughter resounds from the mountain to crest.
When forests exhale, the world joins the jest,
In a world full of whimsy, life's very blessed.

Heartbeats in the Underbrush

Underbrush thumps with a rhythm so light,
As bandits of nature play hide-and-seek right.
A raccoon in disguise, a cheeky, sly chap,
Steals birdseed for breakfast, a real funny rap.

Frogs strike poses, in the mud they all stand,
With jokes on their lips, forming a band.
Tapping their feet as if hosting a show,
Their cackle and croaks steal the fairies' glow.

A fox pulls a prank, oh what a jest,
Confusing a deer—it's nature's best test.
With heartbeats a-flutter, the forest is grand,
In this comedy club, nature's the band.

Twilight descends, shadows weave in and out,
While creatures unite with a jubilant shout.
With laughter and heartbeats that thump in the night,
Underbrush finds joy, every leaf a delight.

www.ingramcontent.com/pod-product-compliance
Lightning Source LLC
Chambersburg PA
CBHW072148200426
43209CB00051B/861